Go
OWN
Yourself!

KELLY BAGLA, ESQ.

UNLEASH YOUR GREATNESS
SO YOU CAN
OWN YOUR WORLD

OTHER BOOKS BY KELLY BAGLA, ESQ.

Go Legal Yourself

Best Seller

What People Are Saying:

A Business Owners Bible – You don't know what You don't know! A must for all business owners or those who want to be!
– By Wes S

Hands down the most amazingly concise and easily comprehensible book that all business owners must read. Having been self-employed for many years this book was purchased by me at an event and it was one that I couldn't put down!

It really made me take stock in my business, how it is structured, what I could improve in and excel to even new heights with respect to my business and taking it to the next level.

It is all about preparation and having a viable business plan and forethought. Things that most entrepreneurs either think they have a handle on or haven't thought about including those that have the appearance of or are extremely successful.

This book is for any business owner large or small. From a sole entrepreneur to a corporation with thousands of employees. I am so impressed that I now use this as my business "go to".

How fortunate and blessed I felt to have been invited to one of the most intelligent business attorneys I have ever met. Kelly Bagla is a force not to be ignored. She CARES genuinely about her clients and is very focused on your success. Completely impressive and not something you just find in today's climate.

Thanks to Attorney Bagla's book I now feel more equipped than most any of my peers on how to structure a road map to keep my business growing and protected. In this current climate we are living in it would be a huge disservice not to purchase this book and implement her amazing strategies for business planning and success.

I also know that Attorney Bagla offers amazing seminars and different levels of support. She truly cares about her clients to the core and I just can't rave about her enough. Truly, if you are a business owner and don't have this book regardless of the stage your business is in you are doing yourself a disservice.

What always seemed a daunting task was actually simplified and made me motivated to make drastic changes to my vision, to my pathway to success and helped me to develop a road map to that success.

Buy this book! It will be the best investment one could ever make as an entrepreneur. It's clever, intelligent, digestible and something I would scream from the roof tops as a must have for business owners.

Since employing her business planning strategies I am seeing an upsurge in my business, have a clear and concise vision as to where I am headed and what I need to do in order to protect myself and company. I generally don't get this excited over these types of reads but I can assure you that you will feel the same way.

Take the plunge, buy this very affordable book and GO SUCCESS YOURSELF! This is a true gem that should be in any business owner's toolbox. And if you ever see that she is doing a seminar or workshop I am quite confident you will want to attend as it will change your life on many levels to include a work-life balance and a clear direction to success.

Kudos to Attorney Bagla for seeing the need for this publication and writing it from the heart with the obvious motivation that she wants entrepreneurs to succeed at every level whether It be a startup or a business that has some tenure.

In any event, don't walk away from success walk toward it and one of the lights shining at the door to success would surely have the cover of this book on its door. Truly inspiring and helpful.

Very good read that will expose the reader to things that… - by Selena R

Very good read that will expose the reader to things that are easily overlooked in the process of establishing a new business or even a growing one for that matter. It embarks on a journey with a four-phase life cycle for your business with key importance of how to protect your business every step of the way. I discovered a lot of things I wouldn't have thought of myself when starting a business. The book is clear, concise, bite size, useful and motivational. Highly recommended!

A quick read packed with useful legal business sense – by LoveLit

Go Legal Yourself is a short but sweet, easy to read and understand Q&A on best practices to avoid pitfalls inherent in launching, growing, maintaining and eventually selling your business. It's definitely a must read for anyone considering starting their own business. It only took me two hours to read. Whether you're just starting out, or managing your own company long term, there is probably something in this quick, concise read you might not have considered that will help you get to the next step. Along with enough DIY information to get you started, Ms. Bagla offers several links to forms and templates available on her website.

Know where you are in your "Legal Lifecycle of your Business" – by J. Biethan

The clarity of "Go Legal Yourself" is priceless! Once I started reading, I never put it down.

If you're considering starting a business (Startup Phase), or in the middle of the Growth Phase, Established Phase or now looking at the Exit Phase - this book is for you!

"Go Legal Yourself" is a road-map to gaining a restful night's sleep from "knowing" what phase of "The Legal Lifecycle Of Your Business" you're in and what you need to consider to maintain its health and your success.

Really, just get a copy

This is one of the best books out there – by Bella B

This is the ultimate blueprint on how to start, own and operate a successful business! Without a doubt, this is one of the best books out there on how to set your business up for success! Whether you're a seasoned business owner or you're just thinking about starting one up, this little gem of a book is an absolute must read! It breaks down and explains the four "legal lifecycles" of a business and thoroughly explains how to find out which phase your business is in and what you need to do in order to protect it. It's a compact, comprehensive guide that shows you exactly what legal documents you need, when you need them, and more importantly, why you need them in order to maximize your profits and protect your assets. "Go Legal Yourself" gives discerning advice on how to operate your business smoothly and effectively. It's a thoughtful, informative and fascinating read! She answers so many questions I never thought to ask. It felt as if someone finally revealed the secret to operating a truly successful business! How refreshing! I hope she writes another book! So, buy this book and "Go Legal Yourself"!

DEDICATION

I dedicate this book to all the self-made leaders.
I am who I am today because I believed in ME!

--Kelly Bagla, Esq.

Special Thanks

Being thankful and expressing your gratitude is an important part of being happy in life.

My first gratitude goes to my loving husband, Brent Waters:
For catching me when I fall
For being there through thick and thin.
For believing in me.
For listening to me.
For hearing my thoughts.
For knowing me inside out.
For never putting me down.
For being my Marine
I love you!

My second gratitude goes to my loving friends, Sally and Richard Crawford:

My dear friends, thank you for walking with me when I needed support.
Thank you for walking ahead of me when I needed guidance.
Thank you for walking behind me when I needed someone to watch my back!

My third gratitude goes to my wonderful clients and associates:

I am truly grateful to you for giving me the opportunity to grow.
None of my achievements would have been possible without your unwavering support.
Thank you for allowing me to be me!

WHY WRITE THIS BOOK?

"Grab the world by the pearls. It's yours for the taking" - Kelly Bagla, Esq.

In the business world, I have heard too many times: "If I can do it...you can do it, too." How many times have you gone to a motivational workshop and the speaker is telling you that they did it and so can you? They began with nothing and now they own a successful business. Let me be the first to tell you that this is the biggest bull you will ever hear! "If I can do it" means I wanted it so bad that I worked hard and was self-driven to achieve what I wanted. You can do it, too, only if you want it that bad and you work hard and stay the course.

I'm a go-getter. Always have been. People have asked me time and time again, "Where do you get your drive?" I have always answered, "My parents taught me to believe in ME." Dad taught me one thing that has never failed me, "If you want something, you must want it from your heart. Otherwise, don't bother!" I would be remiss if I didn't mention, my stubbornness, I get from my mother.

As a self-made woman, I have learned valuable lessons that have made me the leader I am today. These lessons are worth sharing because I know there are other people out there who can become leaders, too, and most of all, want to become leaders. If you have always been told you will never amount to anything and no one believed in you, now is the time to make a change. Now is the time to believe in YOU!

This book is your guide to help you see what's possible, outline objectives to reach your goals, and provide strategies to achieve your dreams. It's your time to grab the world by the pearls because it's YOURS for the taking!

Contents

Go OWN Yourself!

INTRODUCTION

"No price is too high to pay for the privilege of owning yourself." – Friedrich Nietzsche

It's not easy to own yourself in this world. Yes, we are all born free, but what happens when we become adults? To begin with, we're subject to conditioning from our family and society. In most cases, these forces pound us over the head repeatedly, not only to make us conform, but to fully buy into the dominant norms. For Example, if you are a lawyer, you must wear a business suit. If you are a financial advisor, you must wear a business suit. If you are a manager, you must wear a business suit. How do you stand out when you are expected to conform? Do you get where I'm going with this? As part of being a leader you need to stand out so others can recognize you; however, wearing a business suit that everyone else wears is the opposite of standing out.

When you look at your life, you'll notice you have been owned by others, such as, your parents, bosses, and your mentors. You might even have been owned by alcohol, food, or other addictions. This process of being owned can lead to confusion, low self-esteem, and even fear, all states of being that can "make or break" you in the business world.

It's not your fault. Deep inside, you thought you had to do

1

what people told you to do, rather than claim your sovereignty. For many people, self-sovereignty unfolds at an unpredictable pace. They stumble through the challenges of life and learn through experience.

What do I mean by Self-Sovereignty?

- Peeling away layers of conditioning so you can come to know your true self.
- Knowing your true worth.
- Knowing what you want.
- Feeling free of the control, expectations, and coercion of others.
- Knowing your actions have an effect for better or for worse.
- Taking responsibility for your thoughts, words, and actions, aiming for the highest good for yourself and others.
- Feeling grounded in yourself so you're not easily knocked off center when someone makes a suggestion about your life.
- Being self-reliant, but also having confidence to ask for help when needed.

Self-sovereignty is not about self-cherishing, self-absorption, or egotism. It's about removing layers of the false self, so your true self can shine. Then you naturally impact others in the best way possible, as a leader does.

Why do some people wake up one morning and start to own themselves while others never wake up? It could be an unexpected encounter with someone they admire, or a job gone awry that suddenly sets them on a new track. Or maybe they just became fed-up with living someone else's life and wanted to start living their own. Whatever the reason, now is the time to own yourself, otherwise you would never have picked up this book.

For me, I was one of those gifted children who knew with clarity from early on I wanted to live my life in a way that helped others. At the age of five, I knew I wanted to become a lawyer. Now, how the hell did I know that at five? I know, you are probably thinking I'm pulling your leg. Well, hold your judgment as I take you on this journey that led me to owning myself, becoming a leader and living the wonderful life I live today.

Owning yourself makes all the difference in the world in how people perceive you and how you in turn interact with the world. There are only two ways to live. You can glide along and let things happen, reacting to whatever comes your way—good luck, bad luck, whatever the fates happen to serve up. Or, you can choose to own yourself by moving into the driver's seat and intentionally directing the course of your journey. Sound's inspiring, doesn't it? Of course, if you happen to be like most people, already up to your eyeballs with demanding work, commitments, schedules, and a lifetime of emotional baggage, then the idea of suddenly stepping up to take responsibility for your life can seem pretty scary.

To make way for a new attitude about yourself, chances are you are going to have to think differently and accept new ways that can help you become successful in life, not just in your personal life but in your business life. There is no question this can be a daunting task, which is why so many people allow things to remain the same, which leads to a life of untapped potential. This book will help you understand the power you have to choose, to dream, and explore, to determine your course, and to own yourself so you can own your business.

Get ready for a life changing experience as you embark on some inside secrets that make self-made leaders.

Here's to owning yourself!

CHAPTER ONE

KNOW WHO YOU ARE

"Because one believes in oneself, one doesn't try to convince others. Because one is content with oneself, one doesn't need others' approval. Because one accepts oneself, the whole world accepts him or her." – Lao Tzu

Here is a very basic truth: Those who most often get what they want in life take the time to know what they want. As obvious as this may sound, it's surprising how many people never really sit down and do the work to decide what they want from life, not just today, next week, or even next year, but for their whole life. In other words, they are content to take life as it comes.

Some may ask, "What's so wrong with taking life as it comes?" Not a thing; after all, when you are the passenger in a car you get to sit back and enjoy the scenery as you wait to see what comes your way on the journey. But if you want more — more importantly, if you believe you deserve more in life — then you are going to have to take control, get in the driver's seat, and go create your journey.

Every great story has a beginning and here's mine. Growing up with six older siblings I always had the help I needed and the guidance I wanted. Mom and Dad instilled in us all at a very young age that education could open doors for us and that no one would be able to take that away. All my siblings majored in medical related professions, but not me. From the early age of five, I remember all I wanted to be was an attorney. Granted, I had no idea what an attorney was, all I knew was that I wanted to be one.

I was a slow learner in school and I was that kid who had to have things explained a few times before I got it. I was placed in all the lower classes because my slow learning was mistaken for being not very smart. I remember that exact time, like it was yesterday, when I received my very first "A" in English and then in Biology and then in Geography. What changed? My loving sister-in-law started to spend time with me helping me with my homework and the way she explained things made it easy to understand. Something inside of me finally clicked and I not only understood the subjects, but I started to enjoy them. I knew I was somewhat smart, despite what the teachers thought.

I finally went off to college to pursue a degree in business. Why business? Well, when my parents immigrated to England from India, my dad found a job in a clothing factory where he worked on the factory line. Fifteen years later Dad bought out the owner of the clothing factory and became his own boss. This was the first time I was exposed to the business world and I loved everything it stood for. By owning your own business, you are in control of your own destiny; your own work-life balance; you choose the people you want to work with; you reap the rewards because you had the guts to take the risks; and the biggest reason is you get to live your passion. As I saw dad run his business, I learned some very valuable life lessons:

One – If you want something, you go after it with all your heart or don't bother at all.

Two – Believe in yourself and stay the course, because no one else can do it for you.

Three – Don't listen to others who are not vested in your success, this will only lead you to self-doubt.

6

Seeing dad enjoying his business and being the kind of boss a person wanted to work for, I wanted to follow in his footsteps and learn everything I could about business that school could offer.

While at college, I took a business law class, because eventually I did want to go to law school, so I thought I'd get my feet wet. The only thing I remember about that class was I was having a hard time understanding it. My counselor, realizing I was struggling, met with me and encouraged me to pursue a simpler discipline such as liberal arts. But changing disciplines would have led me down a completely different path from what I had planned for myself. I remembered the lessons I learned from Dad. Come hell or high water, I wanted to be an attorney, and I wanted it from my heart. I wasn't about to let the counselor's recommendation be my defining moment. Instead, I retook the business law class, passed with an A- and ended up receiving a Bachelor's degree in Business. With this degree in my pocket, I was off to law school. Eventually, I earned two law degrees, a Bachelor's of Laws and a Masters of Law, and I started my law career with the largest law firm in the world. Not bad for a girl who was a slow learner. I loved my time in that firm because I was exposed to all sorts of cases and I learned from the best attorney minds. The honor of working for the best was a massive achievement for someone that had no help, no advice or mentors, and a person who became the first attorney in her family.

I wanted to become an attorney and I became one. Let me be the first to tell you that it certainly wasn't an easy road. Although my family is very comfortable financially, I couldn't bring myself to ask my parents for money. I put myself through law school by working odd jobs. No, I didn't wait on tables. Although I respect this talent, I knew I wanted to challenge myself. I thought about what I enjoyed doing and started there. I'm a gym rat, always have been. So, I obtained my personal training certificates and I worked as a personal trainer training people from all walks of life. As a personal trainer you need to be comfortable telling people what to do and have them actually follow your advice. I became one of the top sought out personal trainers because I gave people results. This was the first time I realized that I was capable of leading and others were capable of following me.

I also worked as a tax preparer after completing my training and obtaining my license. I must confess, anyone that knows me knows that numbers and I don't get along. That's why I went to law school, but it certainly helps when your husband is a walking calculator. I noticed a pattern regarding the jobs I choose and they all required a challenge. My final job before practicing law was with a Fortune 500 company where I managed 35 international subsidiaries. I had no experience in this field but that didn't stop me. I knew business and I knew this would get me closer to what I really wanted to do, practice business law.

Putting yourself in challenging situations really tests who you are and how much better you can be. Don't go through life being told what to do or doing the same thing you feel comfortable doing. Explore your potential and see where it takes you.

It takes determination and focus to reach your goals and through this process you learn how high you can actually fly. Knowing who you are is critical if you desire to own your place in the world. When you have your own sense of identity you are better able to make decisions and navigate life with more ease. Learning about yourself and developing a solid sense of identity can help you successfully achieve your dreams.

Here are four profound questions you can ask yourself to develop a better sense of who you are and increase self-awareness.

QUESTION 1:

WHAT WOULD YOU BE IF YOU KNEW YOU COULD NOT FAIL?

The risk of failure terrifies most people. How many times have you wanted to change jobs or careers or even own your own business but didn't take the chance because you were too afraid to fail? Failure defines us for the better. When we take a closer look at the great thinkers throughout history, a willingness to take on failure is not a new or extraordinary thought at all. From the likes of Augustine, Darwin and Freud to the business mavericks and sports legends of today, failure is as powerful a tool as any in reaching great success. Without taking the risk, you will never achieve true greatness.

Learn to embrace failure as a friend and learn from the mistakes so those are never repeated. Not everyone who's on top today got there with success after success. More often than not, those best remembered in history were faced with numerous obstacles that forced them to work harder and show more determination than others. Before their success came epic failures. The following is a list of successful people who failed before hitting it big:

Walt Disney - Walt Disney was fired from a newspaper for "not being creative enough," and drove his first business into bankruptcy. When Disney started to think about a full length animated movie, almost nobody else thought this was a good idea. He even had to mortgage his house and take out a loan to finish *Snow White and the Seven Dwarfs* because he ran out of money. When the movie was finally released, it was highly praised by critics and brought in $8 million, making it the most successful sound film made to that date.

Mary Kay - After working 25 years for the same company, Mary Kay made a choice to resign because the company did not accept her ideas. After retirement, she decided to write a book to assist women in business. This book turned into a perfect business plan, and Mary Kay founded the world-renowned cosmetics company that bears her name.

Thomas Edison - Thomas Edison is the best example of how important self-confidence and perseverance are. He failed thousands of times to invent a commercially viable electric light bulb, but to him failure was just another step on the road to success: "I have not failed. I have just found 9,999 ways that do not work." Eventually, Edison produced a bulb that could glow for over 1,500 hours.

Howard Schultz - Thanks to the persistence and tenacity of Howard Schultz, today we can enjoy delicious Starbucks coffee as we work at our computers. It was very difficult for Schultz to convince investors to write him a check. His idea was rejected 214 times before he found someone who believed in it.

Milton Hershey - Milton Hershey worked at a candy factory from a very young age. In 1876, at the age of 18, he opened his first candy shop, but it did not succeed. So, Milton decided to work for another candy factory where he learned much more than he already knew. In 1883, Hershey opened another candy shop which quickly became a success. Ten years later he took a risk and sold his business to start the famous Hershey Chocolate Company.

Stephen King - Stephen King, an American writer began his career with a novel that was rejected 30 times, so he decided to throw it into the garbage. His wife pulled the manuscript out of the trash and convinced him to finish the novel. Finally, *Carrie* was accepted by a publishing house. Stephen King's books have sold more than 350 million copies, many of which have been made into movies.

Michael Jordan - Michael Jordan was cut from his school basketball team. He once said, "I have missed over 9,000 shots in my career. I have lost almost 300 games. On 26 occasions I have been entrusted to take the game winning shot, and I have missed. I have failed over and over and over again in my life. And that is why I succeed."

J. K. Rowling - Before there was a wizard, there was welfare. J. K. Rowling was a broke, depressed, divorced single mother simultaneously writing a novel while studying. Now one of the richest women in the world, Rowling reflects on her early failures:

"It is impossible to live without failing at something, unless you live so cautiously that you might as well not have lived at all, in which case you fail by default."

Elvis Presley - As one of the best-selling artists of all time, Elvis Presley is a household name even years after his death. But back in 1954, Elvis was still a nobody, and Jimmy Denny, manager of the Grand Ole Opry, fired Elvis after just one performance telling him, "You ain't goin' nowhere, son. You ought to go back to drivin' a truck."

Oprah Winfrey - Most people know Oprah Winfrey as one of the most iconic faces on TV as well as one of the richest and most successful women in the world. However, Oprah faced a hard road to get to that position, enduring a rough and often abusive childhood as well as numerous career setbacks including being fired from her job as a television reporter because she was "unfit for TV."

Through failure comes success. Don't be afraid to fail and take that risk.

QUESTION 2:

WHAT ARE YOUR CORE PERSONAL VALUES?

Personal values are the things you believe are important in the way you live your life and the way you do business. They give you a reference for what is good, beneficial, important, useful, desirable, and constructive. Once you determine exactly what values are most important to you, you can better determine your priorities. In fact, having this information about yourself is the key to making sure your daily life is aligned with those values.

Here are seven steps to identifying distinct and meaningful core values:

1. Write down what have been your three greatest accomplishments.

11

2. Write down what have been your three biggest failures.

3. Write down a sentence of advice you would give to yourself based on your answers for the two questions above.

4. Reduce the sentence to a few words to help you narrow your values.

5. Ask your friends or family for words that they would use to describe you.

6. Take a personality test (there are numerous ones online) and see what words are used to describe you.

7. Take all the words used to describe you and narrow them down to about five, then prioritize them.

There are countless types of core values so you will need to choose the ones that are right for you. It's natural to want to choose a long list of core values in an effort to be the best you can be; but limiting your selection to three or four helps you focus on what you stand for. Here are some examples of core values from which you may wish to choose:

- Dependability
- Loyal
- Commitment
- Reliability
- Open-mindedness
- Consistency
- Honesty
- Efficiency
- Innovation
- Motivation
- Good humor
- Compassion
- Optimism
- Passion

- Respect
- Courage
- Education
- Service to others

There is real power in clearly identifying and articulating your core values and making them a prominent behavior driver in your business, career, and in your personal life. Look behind most truly successful people and you will see a set of values that have stood the test of time, such as:

- Accountability
- Commitment
- Loyalty
- Integrity
- Discipline
- Excellence
- Courage

As Mahatma Ghandi said, "Your beliefs become your thoughts. Your thoughts become your words. Your words become your actions. Your actions become your habits. Your habits become your values. Your values become your destiny."

QUESTION 3:

WHAT MAKES YOU GENUINELY HAPPY?

This question is closely related to your core personal values. However, ask yourself this question once you have really nailed down what those values are. For example, if family is one of your core personal values, will building a business that demands 100 percent of your time make you happy? You really need to think about this one because if you don't know what will make you happy, how are you going to own yourself?

Figuring out what makes you happy can be a long process. One way to learn what makes you happy is to gather data throughout your days about how happy you are, so you can notice patterns of happiness. Just for fun, you can take a happiness quiz. You can find any number of these quizzes online. What works for most is actually spending time with yourself, so you are forced to focus on your thoughts and feelings. Some people take long walks to clear their heads, some meditate and some workout. Whatever you do, make sure you actually get in touch with yourself and realize what is happiness to you.

QUESTION 4:

IF MONEY WERE NO OBJECT, HOW WOULD YOU LIVE YOUR LIFE DIFFERENTLY?

Many people equate happiness and success directly to the amount of money they have. This question is not about the money at all. It is more about thinking outside the limits we tend to put on our aspirations and actions because things seem out of reach financially. How many times have you thought about starting a business? How many times have you thought about taking that trip? How many times have you thought about really living the life you want? It may be hard to believe but these things are achievable. Achievement starts with you taking action.

If you promise yourself one thing this year, make it this: today you'll start writing a business plan for the business you have always wanted; or research the trip you have dreamt of enjoying. You may not be able to do those exact things, but once you know what those true dreams are, you expand your thinking and begin to develop a plan to work towards goals you may have never imagined possible.

Don't let money be the barrier between you and the life you want. Become clear on what you want to do with your time on earth and create a plan to get it done. The choice is up to you; however, this question needs to be asked because then you'll know if what you are currently doing is worth it to you.

Knowing who you are is the foundation of who you will become in life. As a society, it seems that we care more about what others think of us then what we think of ourselves. This talks directly to the number two lesson I learnt from dad: Believe in yourself and stay the course, because no one else can do it for you.

The trick to knowing who you are has a lot to do with self-image. As Robert Kiyosaki said, "It's not what you say out of your mouth that determines your life, it's what you whisper to yourself that has the most power!" A self-image is in its most basic form a picture you have of yourself. It's how you think and feel about yourself based on your appearance, performance, and relationships that consistently impact your outlook on life as well as your level of happiness. Your self-image is also the impression you have of yourself that forms a collective representation of your assets and liabilities. In other words, your self-image is how you see yourself based on your strengths and weaknesses. The assets and liabilities often are evident through the labels you give yourself that describe your qualities and characteristics. For instance, you might say:

- I am intelligent
- I am dumb
- I am outgoing
- I am shy

These are just some examples of the many labels you potentially give yourself and the inevitable conclusions you may reach. It is these conclusions you make about yourself that either form the foundation of a healthy self-image or an unhealthy self-image.

If you are going to learn how to own yourself and live the life you want, your goal is to perceive yourself in a healthy way where you are no longer influenced by other people's opinions or by societal expectations. As a result, you will have a more optimistic outlook on life and thereby more confidence in yourself.

In order to have a healthy self-image you must strengthen how you see yourself and strengthening your self-image is simply about doing the small things consistently over time, which will make a big difference in the long run. Here are some ways to start strengthening your self-image:

Don't allow society to define you

Many people walk through life as a passive bystander. They accept how things are and allow society to influence them into thinking and doing things a specific way. Don't let society define you. Start with fully understanding and accepting who you are and then taking charge of the mental processes that are running your life. Start believing in something that matters to you and it is perfectly fine for you to thing and act differently.

Don't indulge in self-judgement or self-criticism

When you judge and overly criticize yourself that is a clear indication that your self-image needs strengthening. Instead of judging or criticizing yourself, choose to give yourself feedback so you can improve, which will help you develop the self confidence you need to build a healthy self-image so you can be the best you can possible be in any situation.

Always follow through with your word

The promises you make to yourself you must keep as kept promises help you create consistency and you need consistency to build a healthy self-image. When you keep your word you are sending a strong message that you are running your life based on your own perspectives and that you are the one in the driver's seat.

Build your self-image upon strong foundations of self-worth

A healthy self-image is built upon the strong foundations of a high level of self-worth, which is how you value and regard you despite what others might say. When you have a high level

16

of self-worth nothing shakes you and when you have a healthy self-image you don't look to outside sources to define who you are.

You and you alone create your own definition of who you are. You and you alone create the impression you have of yourself in each and every situation. You and you alone mold and shape the person you are today and the person you become tomorrow.

"I believe that everything happens for a reason.

People change so that you can learn to let go.

Things go wrong so that you can appreciate them when they're right.

You believe lies so you eventually learn to trust no one but yourself.

And sometimes good things fall apart so better things can fall together." - Unknown

I am not a motivational speaker, but I am an action taker. As you read through this book, I will challenge you to take action, so you can get closer to owning yourself. Following is you first challenge.

Take Action Now

YOUR ASSIGNMENT IS TO ANSWER THE FOLLOWING QUESTION:

What would you be if you knew you could not fail?

_____

_____

_____

_____

_____

_____

_____

_____

_____

_____

_____

_____

_____

18

_____

_____

_____

_____

_____

_____

_____

_____

_____

_____

_____

_____

_____

_____

_____

_____

_____

_____

_____

_____

_____

_____

_____

_____

_____

_____

_____

_____

_____

_____

_____

_____

_____

_____

_____

_____

_____

_____

CHAPTER TWO

KNOW WHAT YOU WANT

"Disciplining yourself to do what you know is right and important, although difficult, is the highroad to pride, self-esteem, and personal satisfaction." – Margaret Thatcher

"I still don't know what I want to be when I grow up." My friend used to say this all the time and she is in her 50s. A lot of people live their lives having no clue what they want. They follow the crowd without a second thought, just because that's what's expected of them. If you ask me, you're probably living someone else's life, because as far as we know, we only have one life to live and at the end you should be able to say:

"I did it my way." – Frank Sinatra.

What do you want? Why is this question hard to answer? Since we are used to playing small, not thinking outside the box and following the rules this question can be overwhelming for some. If you don't know what you really want in life, you're not alone. Thousands, if not millions of people have no clue. Not knowing what you want leads to indecisiveness, which puts you in an endless loop that produces the same old results.

21

How can you find what you want to do in your life? You must understand, the way to what you want is not always a straight path. You need to take a peek into the uncertainty and try new things. This could lead you to becoming clear about what you desire. The need to feel happy is so important because it is one of the first steps towards a better life, filled with self-esteem. If you are still trying to decide what it is you truly want, or even if you think you already know, here are some great questions to ask yourself to see if you have truly figured it out:

WHAT INTERESTS EXCITE YOU THE MOST?

Think about what your real passion and desire is. Too often people are caught up in a life or occupation that they are simply not passionate about. For whatever reason, they wind up doing or being something that they just don't love in an effort to keep the lights on. But in today's society finding and doing something that you're passionate about in life is far simpler than it was just a decade or so ago. Today we can hop online through many means and connect with someone halfway around the world instantaneously. Finding your passion and living it isn't too difficult and it does require some work on your end. If you are willing to deal with the failures and setbacks that might come along with finding and pursuing your passion, then you're in for a lifetime of enjoyment.

So how can you identify and even pursue your passion? It starts with taking the following proactive steps:

Step 1: Build A Rainy-Day Fund

While many people write about finding your passion, the truth is that you can't purse what you're passionate about until you are financially sound and have a rainy-day fund. This means that you have saved up at least six months' worth of savings.

Step 2: Brainstorm

Brainstorm about what you want to do in life by writing down the things that you truly love. Think about what you've been interested in the past. What interest you now? Take as much time brainstorming as possible and find something you truly love to do.

Step 3: Set Goals

Set goals as to what will you do with your life? Where will you live? How will you spend your time? Set a goal for what you want and make sure that goal is strong enough and the meaning is deep enough so that it will propel you forward. When you set your goals be specific about them and go into detail on every aspect of the goal so that you can envision it. Also, make sure you have an exact date on when you'll achieve that goal.

Step 4: Create A Plan

No goal can be fulfilled without a plan. You need to create a roadmap for your life that will map you from where you are to where you want to be. Even if you don't know every step you're going to take, you need a general direction of travel.

Step 5: Take Massive Action

You need to put your plan into place by taking massive action on a daily basis. The best way to take action and ensure that you get things done is to tackle the most important tasks first so you feel like you are making headway.

Step 6: Stay Persistent

It's likely that you may fail a few times while pursuing your passion and that is absolutely fine. If you have a solid plan in place and your rainy-day fund is set, then failure will be more difficult, especially if you are determined.

Remember that anything worthwhile isn't going to come easy. Finding your passion in life and living it every day by doing what you love to do is a dream held by many but fulfilled by few. As long as you don't give up, over time, you can make your dreams come true. It just won't happen overnight. Find your passion means waking up in the morning with a drive and determination to get things done without someone behind you telling you what to do. It requires self-discipline and a desire to achieve more than what we would generally be expected to achieve.

Choosing to do what you like is good for your self-esteem and is the key to your happiness. Once you pinpoint the things you truly enjoy doing, and pay attention to how these motivate you, you may soon notice you have a better idea of what it is you want in life and how you might be able to obtain it. Once you have figured out what excites you the most, I highly suggest you dedicate more of your time to pursue those activities.

What are your biggest successes in life?

No matter how small, list your most important achievements. This will raise your confidence and help you feel better about yourself. Acknowledging your successes is a good place to start because it highlights your talents and strengths and can guide you to where you need to go next. Giving yourself credit for even the simplest of accomplishments can help you feel better and set you up for bigger and better success.

If anything were possible, what would you choose to do and what would you want your life to be like?

This is a big life-changing question, but one that will enable you to start dreaming and imagining the possibilities. If you wish to improve your life, then first you must imagine what is possible. Forget the limits you believe hold you back or stop you, most of these are in your mind and not real limitations. You need to dream big to achieve big.

What are your goals?

Here is where you need to get clear and write your goals down. Do this for as many as come to mind. Think about it, if you have twenty goals and can achieve only ten of them, that's fifty percent. Not bad odds. Your success depends on your ability to think big and to go for it.

WHO IS THE PERSON YOU MOST ADMIRE?

It is important to have a role model, someone to look up to. Having a role model will enable you to understand that you can overcome problems and do what seems impossible, as others have before. You can also understand more about yourself and the values you have because you can see them in the person you have chosen. Ask yourself why you choose that person and you will discover more about who and what you want to be.

HOW WILL YOU COMMIT TO GETTING EVERYTHING YOU WANT?

Once you answer the foregoing questions, you must take action. This is often the hardest step because problems will occur. Two of the biggest problems are fear and doubt. You may require a system of support that works for you when these two problems arrive. Decide how committed you are to making positive changes and be determined to work hard to make them happen. How far will you go if things get tough?

Who can you tell about your plans? Telling someone who you can rely on is important.

If you believe your skills and your talents are in agreement with your desires, search for an activity which reflects them, or create your own. On the other hand, if you believe that you must learn a new skill, then do some research and learn to master it. Any invention, discovery, or business you see in the world, has been created by the human mind. Your mind, too, has endless resources for creativity and will have forever. You will be amazed at how many ideas your mind will give you if you persistently ask these questions of yourself.

You may have passion and enthusiasm, but they alone will not help you succeed if you are lacking the vision for what success looks like. Whether you are 25 or 55, you can make a fresh start and make things happen. However, potential does not equal results. Reaching your dreams will not happen by accident. You must be intentional in making your dreams come true. If you want a fresh start and desire the opportunity to create your own way, you can do it. Anyone can improve their situation. The only thing you can be sure of is that 100 percent of those who do not try will never reach their goals. Most successful people do not focus on the negative, they are both realistic and have an optimistic attitude.

Discovering what you really want to do with your life is not an easy task for anyone, nor is it something that you can create a step-by-step guide for. It will be difficult to answer the foregoing questions but once you have gone through that exercise you might want to also consider asking yourself these questions:

WHERE WILL YOU BE IN FIVE YEARS?

Where will you be in five years is a question that appears in everything from job interviews to financial plans. While it seems cliché, it's common for a reason: It works!

Considering how common a question it is, seeing into the future and picturing where you will be in five years is a lot harder than you think. It does not matter where you think you will be, but it's important to think about because it gives you the idea you want to pursue. Here's a good way to start:

WRITE YOUR PERSONAL MANIFESTO

The idea of a personal manifesto might sound a little silly on the surface. However, if you can figure out where you stand on certain ideas, you might be able to flush out a possible career, business choice, or lifestyle path. Silly or not, personal manifestos have been implemented by everyone from the founders of Google to Frank Lloyd Wright. The point is to give yourself a call to action. It is easy to write your own manifesto, and while you don't have to do it in a specific way, here are a few suggestions for getting started:

Manifestos are most compelling when they are written in the

present tense, as if though the desired outcome is already happening. The best manifestos have three characteristics:

- *They are provocative* – the language of your manifesto should challenge what currently exists.

- *They are grounded* – manifestos cannot be fanciful, they need to be grounded.

- *They are really desired* – manifestos generate results when they reflect something that is truly desired.

A manifesto is meant to motivate, and motivation begins with desire. Here are four steps to write a manifesto:

1. Hold a brainstorming session to identify what you truly want and use Post It Notes to write your ideas down.

2. Identify the most compelling and desired ideas you want by rearranging the Post It Notes from most powerful to inspirational.

3. Create a first draft of your manifesto by writing two or three sentences that really capture the concept by using proactive, grounded, and desired language.

4. Test, revise and publicize your manifesto by first testing it to see if it reflects a real desire, then share it with others to get their feedback, and finally, make it public, which will hold you accountable so you have no choice but to complete your task.

The main purpose of the personal manifesto is to really figure out what you care about, how you perceive yourself, and how you want to act moving forward. Here is an example I wrote a few years back when I was asked: "What sets you apart from other attorneys":

27

"I am a mold-breaker. Each day I help clients raise their horizon by asking positively powerful questions that inspire and point them toward their goals. I turn negativity into inspiring dreams for the future and then equip myself with the resources I need to get the job done."

Volunteer or shadow someone in a business that interests you.

One of the reasons figuring out what you want to do is so terrifying, is you don't know if you can do it. The best way to find out if you even like what you are thinking of doing is to actually do it. Find someone who is doing what you want to do and ask to spend some time with them learning how to do the job. Obviously, job shadowing is tailored to college students, but it is possible for anyone to give it a try, especially if you are willing to work a day or two for free in the industry. To shadow someone, your best bet is to call up a company and set up an appointment. You might be surprised; someone may say yes, and there you'll have it, actual hands-on experience in the industry.

If you want something bad enough, you'll make it happen. However, if you don't want something, even the best of strategies will not serve you. Once you know what you want, taking action and doing what you want is key to moving closer to success.

I am not a motivational speaker, but I am an action taker. I challenge you to take action now, so you can get closer to owning yourself. The next challenge will help you know what you want.

Take Action Now

Your assignment is to write the first page of your manifesto and then share that page with someone you trust.

My Manifesto

_____

_____

_____

_____

_____

_____

_____

_____

_____

_____

_____

_____

_____

_____

_____

_____

_____

_____

_____

_____

_____

_____

_____

_____

_____

_____

_____

_____

_____

_____

_____

_____

_____

_____

_____

_____

_____

_____

_____

_____

_____

_____

_____

_____

_____

_____

_____

_____

_____

_____

_____

CHAPTER 3

KNOW YOUR CONFIDENCE

"Inaction breeds doubt and fear. Action breeds confidence and courage. If you want to conquer fear, do not sit home and think about it. Go out and get busy."
— Dale Carnegie

Confident people are admired by others and inspire confidence in others. They face their fears head-on. They are risk takers. They know that no matter what obstacles come their way, they will get past them. Confident people see their lives in a positive light even when things are not going so well, and they are typically satisfied with and respect themselves. Confidence means being assured of your own worth, ability, and power, regardless of the situation.

Confidence is the most important contributor to performance in the business or personal world. If you are confident, you are going to be motivated, relaxed, focused, and have mostly positive emotions. Confident people inspire confidence in others, their audience, their peers, their bosses, their employees, their customers, and their friends. In contrast, those who lack confidence will likely feel unmotivated, stressed, distracted, and experience mostly negative emotions.

Confidence is extremely important in every aspect of our lives, yet so many people struggle to find it. You don't have to look far to realize that some of the world-famous people lacked confidence, such as Marilyn Monroe, John Lennon, Oprah Winfrey, Angelina Jolie, and Russell Brand to name a few. Yet they went on to achieve great things. Sadly, the struggle can be a vicious cycle, making it difficult for some to achieve success. The good news is that confidence isn't a gift that some are born with and some are not. Confidence can be learned and used as a foundation for success.

A mistake many people make in their understanding of how confidence affects them is to believe that it is something they either have or don't have, and if they don't have it, they will never be able to get it. To the contrary, confidence is a skill developed through awareness and practice linked to knowledge and abilities.

There are numerous resources in books, workshops, and on the Internet to help a person gain confidence. A quick web search brings up dozens of self-help sites touting "100 ways" or "50 steps" to increase confidence. So many options, one can easily be overwhelmed.

Never fear. These methods are all the same basic steps with different nuances. Over the years, by observing my successful clients, I have honed them down to three key strategies to improve confidence:

STRATEGY ONE: CONDITIONING

Conditioning imposes a sense of self-belief. It's an extrinsic, outside-in approach, where you adopt actions to induce confidence in yourself. This is the most popular method within the self-help community. Ever been to motivational seminars or read any self-help books on increasing confidence? Usually they will ask you to do various things like repeat a positive affirmation, pretend that you are already of a certain stature, speak and act confidently, and so on.

Here are some examples of how conditioning increases

confidence:

CONDITIONING - START YOUR DAY BY WAKING UP EARLY

It's amazing the things you get done before the rest of the world is up. I wake up at 3:00 a.m. as that is when my husband has the coffee ready. I spend about one and a half hours of quality time with my family (my husband and three dogs) eating breakfast before I start my day. I'm usually at the gym by 4:30 a.m. and when I'm done, I walk out feeling bullet proof. What an amazing feeling being on top of the world ready to conquer whatever the day brings you. It truly is amazing the brilliant ideas one thinks of while doing cardio. I have had some of my best ideas while sweating away on the stairs. If you need inspiration or feel stuck on solving a problem, you should really try a half hour on any cardio machine and see what happens. After the gym I walk my dogs and I'm in the office by 6:30am.

You have likely heard that successful people are notorious early risers. Here are some examples of successful people you may know that were highlighted in the Huffington Post (www.huffingtonpost.com/entry/this-is-when-successful-people-wake-up):

Apple CEO Tim Cook - wakes up at 3:45 a.m. every morning to go through email, exercise, and grab a coffee before settling in to his work day.

Dwayne "The Rock" Johnson - is already in the gym by 4am to get an edge on the competition.

PepsiCo CEO Indra Nooyi - rises at 4 a.m. and is at work no later than 7 a.m.

Starbucks Executive Howard Schultz - gets up at 4:30 a.m. to walk his dogs, exercise, and then he makes coffee to get the day going.

Jack Dorsey, co-founder and CEO of Twitter and Square -

wakes at 5 a.m. to meditate, exercise, make coffee, and then check in for his work day.

LinkedIn CEO Jeff Weiner - wakes at 5:30 a.m., checks email, reads the news, exercises, meditates, and eats breakfast (all before 9 a.m.).

Richard Branson - rises with the sun at 5:45 a.m. to exercise and eat an early breakfast before work. *Oprah Winfrey* - usually wakes up between 6:02 and 6:20 a.m. and gets her day going by walking the dogs, followed by chai tea or a cappuccino, exercise, meditation, and breakfast.

Warren Buffett - wakes up at 6:45 a.m. and starts his day by reading the newspaper.

Elon Musk - rises at 7 a.m. and begins his day by tackling critical emails, and then gets his kids off to school, showers, and heads to the office.

Amazon Founder and CEO Jeff Bezos - prioritizes 8 hours of sleep and usually gets his day started between 7 and 8 a.m., reading the newspaper while exercising on the treadmill.

Attacking the day on your own terms, first-thing, also gives you a sense of control in your life. Early morning hours enable you to play offense, instead of being reactive to emails, calls, meeting, and other demands on your time.

CONDITIONING - EXERCISE IN THE MORNING SO YOU FEEL BULLET PROOF ALL DAY LONG.

Pick an exercise you enjoy doing. Make that time all about you with no distractions. Everything else can wait until you are done. While working out at the gym I never bring my cell phone. Gym time is for me.

As mentioned before, you will be surprised to find when

you're focused on exercising to better yourself, you will do some of your best thinking. Set time aside and give yourself goals you're actively working towards, whether it's losing weight or running a certain distance. Practicing discipline as you work out and seeing results will help you carry that into your personal and business life.

It is often publicized that many of the Fortune 500 and the most innovative companies in the world including Google, Apple, and even Deloitte have onsite exercise facilities. Science shows that less than one hour a day of physical activity can improve your health, boost your mind, and help you be more productive. Indeed, people who exercise regularly develop brain skills, have a more positive outlook on life, and are able to better balance between business and family.

Here are five ways exercise can help you succeed:

1. Reduce stress by bumping up the production or your brain's endorphins.
2. Improve sleep by reducing the time it takes to fall asleep.
3. Increase energy by releasing endorphins to raise energy levels.
4. Develop discipline by changing the brain in ways to improve memory and thinking skills.
5. Define and protect "me" time.

CONDITIONING - DRESS TO IMPRESS

Before you leave the house for business, make sure you look the part. We have all heard the saying: *Dress for the job you want, not the job you have.* Your style reflects what you and your company project. Everyone is going to have their own look, but this look should be comfortable and powerful. First impressions are the number one thing that could make or break your deal, and usually within the first five seconds someone has already made up their mind about you. Although, I am an attorney and it is "required" in my profession to wear a suit, you will never see me in one. I feel uncomfortable and out of place in a suit; besides, I have not come across a women's suit that fits right or that does not look blocky. I wear professional looking dresses and accessorize accordingly and that makes me feel confident and powerful because I own that look! People remember me by the way I dress and always pay me complements. In fact, a business woman once told me that I should go into fashion rather than law. I responded by saying: "Why can't I do both?" Owning your look defiantly helps you stand out from the rest.

We all should dress to impress and to make things easy, here are some guidelines for making a good impression on just about anyone, in just about any scenario:

At a job interview – Always wear a nice suit with a tie for men, and a nice business dress for women. These types of clothing project professionalism and suggest that you know your material, even before you open your mouth.

At a networking event – If you are meeting with contacts outside the office, you will want people to approach and remember you. You should look professional and polished without fading unmemorable into the crowd. For men, this is a good time to wear a colorful tie, which could be a conversation starter. For women, you may want to wear an eye-catching statement necklace, which will leave a lasting, professional impression.

As a public speaker – Whether you're addressing an audience of hundreds, presenting to a board of twenty, or moderating a panel of five, what you wear to speak in public should portray a powerful you. As a general rule, you want to be as dressed-up as the best-dressed person in the room. You want to stand out so people can recognize you and remember you after your speech. Solid colors are best for projecting authority and you can never go wrong wearing red. For men, a red tie and for women, a red dress. Red resembles power, authority, and shows you are in control. (By the way, red is my favorite color.)

CONDITIONING - PAY ATTENTION TO YOUR BODY LANGUAGE

Body language speaks to your confidence level. If someone were to walk in the room right now, what preconceptions might they make about you simply based on your body language? If you don't think your body has a language of its own, think again. A large percentage of communication and how people perceive you comes from body language. This includes posture, gestures, facial expressions, and eye movements.

A confident person will carry themselves in a manner that projects authority; they command the room, and they do so by making it look effortless. Here are some powerful body language tips which can instantly boost your confidence:

- Practice good posture by walking or sitting upright. Working out always helps with good posture.
- Use power poses. Adopt stances associated with confidence, power, and achievement, such as standing or sitting upright, head held high, arms either open or propped on the hips.
- Have a strong handshake, as it is a universal sign of strength and assuredness.
- Make eye contact to show you are engaged and genuinely interested in what someone has to say.
- Practice smiling to show you are approachable and likable.
- Dress with confidence but make sure you are comfortable in your choice of attire. Don't forget the statement pieces.

CONDITIONING - ENGAGE YOUR BRAINPOWER

Practicing mental techniques such as positive thinking is a great way to gain confidence, focusing on your strengths rather than weaknesses, and visualizing positive outcomes. Confidence is the cornerstone of success. If you don't believe in yourself, how do you expect others to believe in you? Here are seven ways FBI agents learn to boost their confidence, and if it's good enough for our finest, it's good enough for you:

Push through self-limiting beliefs – Find your limits by exposing yourself to different situations and pushing through the uncomfortable. Once you have confidence in yourself, you'll be amazed what you can accomplish.

Never confuse memory with facts – Revisit the facts of a memory loaded with self-limiting beliefs and try to gain a more accurate perspective on the event.

Talk to yourself – Be positive, because the way you talk to yourself influences your neurobiological response to how others talk to you When you say, I know what to do here or see things as a challenge rather than a problem, you've turned your response into a positive one.

Think positive to overcome your negativity – Negative thoughts drain you of energy and keep you from being in the present moment. Sometimes we will allow our negative past to creep into the present and we start believing we can't do that or this, so why bother. Thinking positively can reassure you to take a risk and try something that you have always wanted, despite the fact that everyone else thinks it's a bad idea and therefore you do, too. Break free from the negative thoughts and focus on your positive self. Never say never until you have tried it.

Raise your curiosity level – Ask questions and be curious because it keeps your mind active instead of passive and it opens up new worlds and possibilities.

Overcome self-doubt – No one but you is stopping you from achieving what you want to accomplish. It's time to identify the areas in which you doubt yourself and remove those barriers.

Face your fears – When we feel in control, we're not afraid. When we have a level of comfort with something, it's not scary. Confront your fears and spend time with them, as you will realize that your fear was all in your mind.

STRATEGY TWO: PERFECTING YOUR CAPABILITIES

The second strategy is working on issues that threaten your self-confidence. As mentioned earlier, confidence is often linked with possessing certain knowledge, skills, and abilities. Many people lack confidence because they feel they lack a certain competency. For example, if you lack confidence about your role in a job, it may be because you lack the information and know-how to perform well. People with a high level of competency in a certain area often develop high self-confidence in that area as a result.

I remember when I first passed the bar exam, I was a fresh young lawyer with bright eyes and bushy tail wanting to learn everything. It was easy to get intimidated by the senior lawyers; many of us new lawyers did. Once I became more knowledgeable about the law, my confidence level changed. I realized that I had the same license to practice law as the senior lawyers did, and the only difference was the years of practice. There really was nothing to be intimidated about.

The first step to increasing your personal and professional competence is to understand you have room for improvement. If you believe you have no room to grow, you will not grow. Once you see there are areas for improvement in your life, growing your competence in those areas is quite simple.

Here are a few quick and easy ideas for growing your competence:

Consider every circumstance an opportunity. Napoleon Hill said, "Every adversity brings with it the seed of an equivalent advantage." If you are willing to see every conflict, every delay, and every frustration in this light, your whole life becomes a learning opportunity. Consider how many times some of the most successful people in the world have failed before making it big:

Abraham Lincoln

- Lost his job at age 23
- Lost his bid for State Legislature
- Lost the love of his life
- Lost his bid to become Speaker in the Illinois House of Representatives

Albert Einstein

- Failed to pass the examination for entrance into the Swill Federal Polytechnic school
- Saw himself as a failed son to his parents
- Sold insurance door-to-door.

Winston Churchill

- Failed the entry exam twice to the Royal Military College
- Lost a total of five elections
- Had trouble speaking and making speeches.

Sylvester Stallone

- Sold his dog for $25 to pay his electricity bill
- Rejected 1,500 times by talent scouts, agents and everyone in the film industry
- Slept in the New Jersey Port Authority bus terminal for three weeks.

Join a mastermind group. The power of a group is hard to argue. Surround yourself with people who are more successful, more competent, and more qualified than you. The benefits you will receive are:

- You will create deep and lasting connection with some

incredible people.

- You will be challenged.
- You will be held accountable.
- Groups are a great place to brainstorm new and old ideas.
- Receive support and feedback.
- You will be encouraged to think bigger.

Use time wisely. So much time in our day is wasted doing mindless things: watching TV, checking social media, sitting in traffic, or waiting for a meeting to start. Set yourself up to take advantage of those moments by listening to podcasts in the car or loading books onto your computer or phone for those down moments. Some of the benefits are:

- You'll become more imaginative.
- You can learn new things.
- You will become a better listener.
- Gain new interests.
- Explore the world.

It's amazing how much you can change your life by simply spending fifteen to twenty minutes a day listening to something powerful that can help you become the best you, either in business or your personal life.

STRATEGY THREE: KNOW YOUR WORTH

The third strategy in building your confidence is knowing your worth. Babies are born knowing their worth and as life moves on, the comments, expectations, and attitudes of other people can wear down this natural sense of self-worth. Self-worth is what enables us to believe we are capable of doing our best with our talents, of contributing well in society, and we deserve to lead a fulfilling life. If you don't know your value, you'll settle. You will undercharge, get pushed around, and dream small. That's why knowing your worth is so important, not just in business, but in life.

Here are some tips on building your worth that have been proven to work:

Understand the power of your attitude toward yourself. The only way we can change is if we choose to change. We all want good results from the effort that we put forth. For the most part, we are willing to put in the necessary hard work. What a lot of us do not know is that we have it in us to put our potential into action and reach the result we desire. There is a single attribute that will determine the level of our potential and will predict the outcome of our effort, and that is attitude.

How you perceive yourself, how you talk about yourself, and how you represent yourself eventually become the reality of you. And if it happens that you're putting yourself down, belittling your worth, and making light of your talents in the face of others, then others will put you down and belittle you too. By choosing to have a positive attitude rather than a negative attitude, you can change your life.

The beauty of attitude is that it can be changed. You need to start thinking differently about yourself, and I understand it might be hard if you have spent years underestimating your worth, but it is always possible to change your thoughts and to learn to value yourself. This reminds me of a particular conversation I had with a few acquaintances a while back. They found it hard to accept complements from others and at that time I could not understand why. When someone would say, "nice dress" or "nice shoes" they would deflect and say "Oh, I've had it for a while." They could not bring themselves to simply say, "Thank you." This is a prime example of underestimating your worth. Start by thinking you are a valuable person, equal to everyone else, and that your talents and thoughts are unique and worthy.

Trust your own feelings. Self-worth requires you to learn to listen to and rely on your own feelings and not automatically respond to the feelings of other people. Self-worth plummets when you let others make decisions for you. Initially this may seem like the easy route and one that allows you to avoid hard choices. Consider the benefits of trusting your feelings:

- Your intuition helps identify your true mission. Following your dreams and being clear in what you want will move you faster to your definition of success.
- When you listen to your intuition you become open to new ideas that perhaps you were limiting yourself from thinking. Your intuition helps you see new things you otherwise would have been closed off to.
- Using your intuition allows you to sense when things are off in your personal or business life. Intuition enables you to tweak your approach and maintain a successful relationship.

The truth of the matter is, there is one person who will never let you down and that is *you*, because you trusted your feelings. So, start trusting your own feelings. It is perfectly fine to talk to others about your decision but ultimately you will need to be the one that makes that decision.

Analyze yourself. Many of us live in a culture which values going to see someone else to analyze us. Unless you've got a serious disorder, garden-variety uncertainty and lack of purpose does not need analysis by someone else. It needs self-analysis so that you can clearly recognize where you're underestimating yourself. Consider the benefits:

- Leads to self-improvement
- Leads to better decision making
- Leads to considering other options
- Leads to dreaming big.

Start by asking yourself what experience have I had? How has this experience enhanced my growth? What are my talents? What are my skills? What are my strengths? What do I want to be doing in life? What makes me feel fulfilled? You will be surprised to some of the answers to these questions and you'll soon realize that your worth just went up.

"There is one irrefutable law of the universe: We are each responsible for our own life. If you're holding anyone else accountable for your happiness, you're wasting your time. You must be fearless enough to give yourself the love you didn't receive." – Oprah Winfrey

I am not a motivational speaker, but I am an action taker. I challenge you to take action now, so you can get closer to owning yourself. The next challenge is going to push you, but it will help you with knowing your confidence.

Take Action Now

Your assignment is to wake up before 6 a.m. and work out, and while working out, think of one idea you can implement in business or life.

My Workout Ideas:

_____

_____

_____

_____

_____

_____

_____

_____

_____

_____

_____

_____

_____

_____

GO OWN YOURSELF

CHAPTER FOUR

KNOW HOW TO COMPETE

"You don't overcome challenges by making them smaller but by making yourself bigger." – John C. Maxwell

Our world loves to compete. We measure success based on the accomplishments of others. We compare the type of business we own, the neighborhood we live in, the car we drive, even the schools we have attended. We compare our job titles, our salary, our savings account, even our retirement age. Unfortunately, these comparisons rarely bring any joy into our lives. One reason is because comparisons by their very nature are unfair. We know ourselves better than we know others. As a result, we compare the worst we know of ourselves to the best we assume in others.

Being competitive has gotten a bad reputation. Instead of associating competitiveness with ambition and betterment, we associate it with ruthlessness, and the idea that you are out for yourself. The truth is, even the most team-oriented and giving people can be the most inherently competitive. Being gracious and supportive, and also being competitive, are not mutually exclusive personality traits.

Too much time and energy can be spent worrying about what other people have and what other people have accomplished. People who have mastered the balance between being competitive and supportive have learned to funnel that energy. Rather than compete with other people, they compete with themselves. The world's best athletes set their first priority as competing against themselves and trying to improve their previous performance.

BENEFITS OF COMPETING WITH YOURSELF

Competing with yourself forces you to take responsibility for what you *can* control, and what an incredible feeling it is.

Competing with yourself eliminates unnecessary worry and stress. Each of us should be focused on creating a life that is inherently congruent with our passions and values.

Competing with yourself enables you to realize your full potential. It is fine to look at others to see what is possible, but you can still push for your own personal successes. Your success will be unique to you and your abilities. What you will discover, if you keep working and refuse to give up, is you are more capable than you ever imagined, and this allows you to reach your true potential.

Competing with yourself unleashes all sorts of greatness that you never thought you had. Here are some more reasons to compete with yourself:

- You define the measure of your success.
- You get a better sense of what you are capable.
- You embrace more of the unknown.
- You get to define your own success.

WHAT DOES IT TAKE TO COMPETE WITH YOURSELF AND ACTUALLY GET RESULTS?

Results take motivation and ability. One of the best ways to improve your personal effectiveness is to master your motivation and find your drive. If you can master motivation, you can deal with life's setbacks, inspire yourself to always find a way forward, create new experiences for yourself, and follow your growth.

According to the research of Dr. Anders Ericsson, motivation is the most significant predictor of success. Motivated people are determined to do whatever is necessary to achieve their goals. They possess a growth mindset, and their desire to succeed trumps any challenge that stands in their way. All we must do is look at successful people around us and ask, what contributes to their success? It's all about motivation.

Here are some proven tips that successful people use to keep them motivated:

Set goals. A lot of us have goals, and some of us actually write them down. The more specific you get with your goals, the more achievable they become. For example, instead of saying you want to have a booming business or to own a home, start by saying you plan to develop a sound business plan, or put $1,000 away in your savings every month. Create short-term goals that are to the point, are tangible, and within your reach.

Create an action plan. Successful people know what it takes to reach their goals, and they create a plan of action that will serve as the roadmap to get them there. If your goal is to create a business plan, your plan of action should include writing a summary of your business idea, researching your target market, researching your competition, looking at different marketing strategies, researching different financing options, and so on.

Create a schedule. The trick to staying motivated and getting things done is scheduling. Take it from a busy attorney, using a to-do list is a tool that keeps you on track. Break down your day and schedule *everything*. For example, pencil in time to exercise, walk the dog, make phone calls, and run errands. It may seem tedious, but scheduling will really help structure your day and get things done.

Use an accountability partner. Peer pressure can be a wonderful thing for motivation. Share your goals with an accountability partner, such as a business coach, or a friend that can stay on top of you. If nothing else gets you moving, having someone continually check up on you or ask you how you're doing with your goals will.

Reframe negative situations. We all have setbacks. We sometimes even completely fail. But successful people don't let setbacks stop them. Instead, they reframe the situation and look at it differently. Rather than spending time reflecting on what they did wrong and how they failed, they spend time thinking about what they could have done differently and how to improve the next time around.

Visualize the future. Successful people think about what they want to achieve and look at the bigger picture. Keep your goals in mind, visualize them, and stay motivated to achieve them. If you can see it, you can achieve it.

Have fun. If you are not having any fun, chances are you are not going to be motivated to do great things. If you take everything seriously, you are going to start resenting your goals and may even discard them completely. Challenge yourself to get things done faster and more efficiently and remember to do something fun each day as a reward for finishing your tasks.

If you truly want to become better at what you do, then it's time you change your mind about what it means to compete and win. We have become so careful about protecting people from losing, we have forgotten the true meaning of what it means to win. It is important to understand that to win, you need to first compete with yourself, and win against the goals you set for yourself. Winning is giving one hundred percent of your effort in preparation for and during your competition, regardless of the circumstances facing you. A person can be a winner as long as they give everything they've got.

Here are some strategies you can practice to maintain your passion and excitement, and be fired up about competing with yourself and winning:

Get started. One of the easiest things you can do to motivate yourself is to think of the work as not being hard. Make a decision to go all the way. Up to now, you have thought about it, but now make up your mind and by deciding to be the best you can at what you do, your life will take off. Just get started.

Take control. While it's easy to be overwhelmed by various personal and professional responsibilities, you can help yourself stay focused by keeping in mind that you are in control of your own actions. If something does not work, you have the ability to change it and start again. Sometimes visualizing the short-term and the long-term benefits can help you see a clearer picture.

Surround yourself with other people who are working hard. To pursue your goals with everything you have, it's helpful to be around other people who are working just as hard. Whether it's your employees or coworkers who inspire you on the job or a group of like-minded professionals you meet with, it's important to have peers who push you to succeed.

Break up tasks into smaller tasks. How do you eat an elephant? One bite at a time. (Just for the record, I love elephants and they should never be eaten.) Breaking your work into parts makes it easier to see where the obstacles are so you can be prepared to overcome them. Indeed, it's important not only to identify these small tasks, but to pat yourself on the back when you complete them.

Stay focused. It's difficult to motivate yourself to keep working if you are not able to concentrate on the task at hand. Limit your exposure to outside distractions by setting time aside to do the task and not letting anything else distract you within that time frame.

Remember your why. Nothing is more motivating than reminding yourself why you are doing the work in the first place. Whether you are building a business you love or simply putting food on the table for your family, it is crucial that you remain in touch with what inspires you.

You have heard that adage, "Practice as if you are the worst and compete as if you are the best." The best way to beat the competition is to compete against yourself. Believe in your capability, your caliber, and your performance. Work your way hard enough, set goals that you think you should achieve not what you think you can achieve and start competing with yourself every day. Remind yourself that competing with yourself is about being better than you were the day before.

"To be a champion, compete; to be a great champion, compete with the best; but to be the greatest champion, compete with yourself." – Matshona Dhliwayo

"You have competition every day because you set such high standards for yourself that you have to go out every day and live up to that." – Michael Jordan

"I'm not in competition with anybody but myself. My goal is to beat my last performance." – Celine Dion

"When we are in competition with ourselves and match our todays against our yesterdays, we derive encouragement from past misfortunes and blemishes. Moreover, the competition with ourselves leaves unimpaired our benevolence toward our fellow men" – Eric Hoffer

"Life is not a competition with others. In its truest sense it is rivalry with ourselves. We should each day seek to break the record of our yesterday. We should seek each day to live stronger, better, truer lives; each day to master some weakness of yesterday; each day to repair past follies; each day to surpass ourselves. This is, simply, progress." – C. Smith Sumner

True skills are only born from trying, doing and creating. Falling in the process is natural as knowing you can pick yourself up and you will survive and eventually thrive. If you ever doubt yourself or where you are heading, close your eyes, picture yourself on the edge of a precipice. See your wonderful future in front of you, touch it and then get behind yourself to achieve.

So, when I look back on my life and look at all the times I failed, I fell and I floundered the voice in my head from my Dad rang true over and over again. It was up to me to pick myself up, assess how to resolve the damage and push myself to new beginnings.

I am not a motivational speaker, but I am an action taker. I challenge you to take action now, so you can get closer to owning yourself. The following challenge will help you with knowing how to compete.

Take Action Now

Your assignment is to pick one thing you do daily for your business and take it to the next level by doing it better tomorrow. It can be anything. After tomorrow, take it to the level above that, and so on until you are the best at it.

One thing to improve day after day:

_____

_____

_____

_____

_____

_____

_____

_____

_____

_____

_____

_____

_____

_____

_____

_____

_____
_____
_____
_____
_____
_____
_____
_____
_____
_____
_____
_____
_____
_____
_____
_____
_____
_____
_____

CHAPTER FIVE

KNOW HOW TO STAND OUT

"Why blend in when you were born to stand out?"
— Guru Granth Sahib

Why do we work so hard to fit in, when we were born to stand out? You give your best, perform well and hope it gets you noticed, but while good performance is important and critical to advancing personally and in business, unfortunately, it's not always enough. So, how do you make sure people remember you? How do you make a solid lasting impression? What makes you different and how can you stand out from all the rest? Sometimes a massive difference is not required, but a noticeable one is. Often the simplest differentiation can be the key to establishing your brilliance.

It can be as small as paying attention to what you already do, or it can be as large as practicing the following differentiators:

Attitude. Wherever you are, be enthusiastic, be positive, be engaging and be passionate. An upbeat, professional attitude stands out. No matter what the day brings, it's important to show that you can stay confident and upbeat. People generally enjoy working with others who are pleasant, encouraging, and constructive, rather than complaining, negative, rude, and destructive. When I walk into the gym at 4:30 a.m., I'm smiling and greet people with happy energy, while others drag themselves around because it's too early. When I'm asked how I am, I always say "I'm fantastic." Being consistent can also help with having a positive attitude.

Engagement. Be approachable, friendly, and show your personality. Build genuine relationships and trust by engaging others and showing an interest in their lives. Everyone loves to hear their name so use their name when speaking and genuinely pay attention. As an attorney I meet a lot of people, from the person serving me coffee to CEOs. I always engage and address them by their name to show that I genuinely care how their day is going. It certainly doesn't hurt if you engage in an English accent! I was born and raised in England and have never lost my accent.

Communication. You might think excellent professional communication skills is something you're born with, but you'd be mistaken. Many competent people lack effective, professional communication skills. Pay careful attention to how you express yourself, not only in formal written communications, but also in emails, on the phone, and in face-to-face conversations. As an attorney I am often confronted with adverse situations but I always remain claim and respectful. Be confident, respectful, and clear in all your communications. Developing stellar communication habits goes a long way towards differentiating yourself. You may want to explore some courses on how to become an effective communicator. It will really serve you well.

Contribution. Dedication and involvement stand out. Be more prepared, do your homework, gather your resources, and show up ready to impress. Such actions will pay off as your clients, peers and friends will notice and remember you as the one who knows their stuff. Prior to meeting with new people, I always gather as much information on them as I can so they know I took the meeting seriously.

Creative thinking. Don't be afraid to express your creativity and look for innovative solutions. Ask intelligent and useful questions and ask questions that no one else is asking. It's often not the answers you provide that make an impression, but your ability to ask insightful questions.

There really are no stupid questions but some thought must be put into them.

Results. Results speak very loudly for themselves. People pay more attention to what you do than what you say. Strive to be the go-to person whenever your skill is needed. Don't hesitate to toot your own horn occasionally. There's nothing wrong with letting people know when you've achieved something significant.

Sometimes we just want to look and sound like everyone else, to wear the same clothes, listen to the same music, and buy the same things. As social beings, we are inclined to want to blend in with everyone else, conforming to their values and ideas. We feel that there is safety in numbers and if everyone else is acting a certain way, then it must be okay. However, to maximize your true potential, you need to stand out from the crowd.

Here are ten reasons why you need to stand out:

1. The masses are mediocre, and you are capable of more.
2. You cannot be a leader if no one can tell you apart from those who are supposed to be following you.
3. You are unique, with unique skills, experiences and ideas, so don't waste that by being the same as everyone else.

4. No one ever achieved greatness or made a difference by conforming to the standard of the people around them.
5. The longer you conform to the crowd's requirements, the harder it is to break away when you need to.
6. The masses are generally fearful and suspicious; being bold and fearless is a much more rewarding and

exhilarating way to live.
7. The crowd has low energy levels; standing out through excellence, innovation, or optimism gives you passion for living.
8. Great people make it happen, and average people let it happen.
9. Be remembered for who you are and not who you looked like and followed.

As far as we know, you only have one life to live. Make it your life that you live and not the masses.

Successful people never blend in, and it is by design. Here are some habits successful people adopt:

- They have an incredible amount of faith
- They think abundantly
- They constantly invest in themselves
- They work according to a life plan
- They lead a balanced lifestyle
- They treat people with respect
- They focus on their strengths
- They are transparent
- They manage their time
- They manage their money
- They constantly challenge themselves
- They are grateful

IF YOU ARE LOOKING TO GET AHEAD, YOU MUST STAND OUT FROM THE CROWD

Standing out is critical to business success, but it is key to succeeding as an individual, as well. The only way to stand out is to do it, and you can do it by incorporating these tips:

Use your strengths. One thing all people who stand out have in common is an in-depth knowledge of their strengths. Great brands are built around strengths. The Ritz Carlton is known for the finest customer service. If you stay in their rooms, you probably won't pay much attention to the furniture and design, which are nice but not remarkable. But the service will be unforgettable. Volvo builds their brand around safety. Their cars may not be the sexiest but they are renowned for being among the safest. W Hotels builds its brand around being trendy and trendy is what you get at every one of their hotels. If you follow a similar approach and maximize your strengths you will stand out.

Know yourself. Get feedback from others and learn as much as you can about how you come across in a private and public setting. The feedback might surprise you. Maybe you come across shy, maybe you don't smile or make eye contact, or maybe you just need to change your body language. Then you can accurately target how you appear in a crowd and what you need to work on.

Take yourself seriously. Being a passionate person, an entrepreneur, leader or business owner requires that you become a master at your craft. It means being competent at the things you do, constantly honing and developing your skills in every way possible. When you take yourself seriously, so do others.

Have a confident exterior. It's important to feel confident; when a person stands out, their confidence shows. Start with the foundation, your posture, by standing up straight. Second, look the part: dress well, look professional, style your hair. Finally, make sure your body language is strong and direct. When talking to people, look them in the eye and extend a firm handshake. Physicality and appearances go a long way.

Voice your ideas. People who stand out are willing to speak their mind, even if this means taking a risk. Approach it from a respectable place but say what you have to say. Chances are someone is thinking the exact same thing as you but hasn't found the courage to voice it.

Get Specific. It is hard to be successful if you don't know what you're trying to succeed at, so get specific. Figure out exactly what you are trying to achieve and break it down into the steps you need to make it happen. For example, instead of focusing on starting your own business, start with developing your business plan this month. If you want to travel to Scotland, start by examining your budget and allocating part of your monthly income to savings.

Practice what you preach. Make sure that everything you do, how you show up, how you act, what you say, what you do is a reflection of who you are, so your character is consistent across every situation.

"The one who follows the crowd will usually go no further than the crowd. Those who walk alone are likely to find themselves in places no one has ever been before." While this quote has been credited to everyone from Francis Phillip Wernig to Einstein himself, the powerful message does not lose its substance no matter whom you chose to credit. From your personal life to your business, copying what your competitors are doing and failing to forge your own path can be a detrimental mistake.

Great things can happen when you set yourself up to be noticed in the right ways. Practice these tips and you'll not only stand out in the crowd but probably travel far beyond it.

I am not a motivational speaker, but I am an action taker. I challenge you to take action now, so you can get closer to owning yourself. The following challenge will help you with knowing how to stand out.

Take Action Now

Your assignment is to find one thing that will help you stand out, be it dressing differently or adopting a positive attitude wherever you are at any given time.

How I Stand Out:

_____

_____

_____

_____

_____

_____

_____

_____

_____

_____

_____

_____

_____

_____

_____

_____

_____

_____

_____

_____

_____

_____

_____

_____

_____

_____

_____

_____

_____

_____

_____

_____

_____

_____

GO OWN YOURSELF

CHAPTER SIX

Know How to Become a Leader

"Look at a day when you are supremely satisfied at the end. It's not a day when you lounge around doing nothing; it's when you've had everything to do, and you've done it."
—Margaret Thatcher

If you Google the word *leadership* you can get about 479,000,000 results; each definition as unique as an individual leader. It's a difficult concept to define, perhaps because it means many things to different people. A simple definition is that leadership is the art of motivating a group of people to act towards achieving a common goal. Being a leader is difficult, but not impossible. There is no inborn quality that leaders possess. They actually are ordinary people who decide at one point to do extraordinary things.

Each of us believe we have a good idea about what it means to be a good leader. For some, leadership is motivation, for others, it equals results, for others it is inspiration. I like to define leadership by narrowing down the description and highlighting the important qualities that makes a leader. The following is a list of qualities that a good leader should possess. As you read these qualities, think of a leader as not just a CEO of a company, but anyone who wants to make a difference in the lives of others.

Vision. The very essence of leadership is that you must have a vision. It's got to be a vision you can articulate clearly. Good business leaders create a vision, articulate the vision, passionately own the vision, and drive it to completion.

Motivation. The leader knows how to motivate better than anyone else. It is one of their main functions. Through motivation, the leader channels the energy and professional potential of their coworkers or team to achieve the objectives.

Serving. The leader is at the service of the team, and not the other way around. The team must have and feel the support of their leader, the tools needed to do their jobs properly must be available to them, and they must give recognition for their efforts.

Creativity. The definition of leadership also has to do with creativity. Good leaders create an environment that will encourage all the members of their team to develop their skills and imagination, so that they can contribute to the common project and vision. If you want to lead successfully, respect the creativity of others, and learn from the people around you, their ideas will surely prove to be positive for you.

Thoroughness. A good leader sets the bar high for their people because they want to reach the goals and make the best of their team. Only a demanding leader will achieve great results. In addition to this thoroughness, the leader must know how to listen, understand the needs of the team, and then provide the necessary time and resources for them to do their job properly.

Empathy. While a leader must be rational, they almost must develop a keen sense of empathy. A leader that can empathize will have a better sense of the team's problems and fears and therefore might be more successful in alleviating them.

Managing. Pure management focuses on the tasks, real leadership focuses on the people. The leader must be at the forefront to lead and guide their team throughout the whole process until the goal is reached. But besides being that torchbearer, leaders also know when to step back and allow their team to take the initiative. In this way, the team gets the chance to develop, both personally and professionally.

Taking risks. The leader is the one responsible for taking the risks that others are not willing to take. They are confident enough to make a decision, and if they make a mistake, the leader must have the courage to rectify it, assume their guilt, and take the right path, without blaming it on the team. Good leaders know how to get ahead of their time, they see opportunities where others cannot, and know how to spread the enthusiasm for their vision to try to make it real.

Improving. True leadership seeks continuous improvement. Leaders turn the people in their teams into stars, people who have improved and developed their skills through the influence of their leader.

Whether you aspire to be an entrepreneur or a CEO of a large company, you should set your goals high and actively work on becoming a stronger leader. Here are ten steps that can help get you started on the path to success:

1. *Learn from your failures.* Great leaders learn from their mistakes. We have all made them but learning from them makes you a better person rather than a person who just made a mistake. Analyzing what went wrong is a tried and tested way to help prevent it from happening again.

2. *Accept responsibility.* Leaders give others due credit for successes and take responsibility for their own shortcomings and failures.

3. *Groom your successors.* Developing a new generation of leaders is essential to your success. You cannot climb higher if there is no one to take your place, so do not be afraid to delegate responsibilities and groom your

73

successors. Giving up control is a sign of a confident leader.

4. **Provide direction.** Achieving business or personal goals require hard work and collaboration. As a leader, it's your job to motivate your people to work toward the common goals. It takes time and energy to learn what motivates each person, but that is what a true leader does.

5. **Be trustworthy.** Many people have problems giving trust to others in general. To earn this trust from others, it will help to be honest and transparent. Always stick to your word.

6. **Be authentic.** If possible, try to stay in touch with your inner real self. Recognizing both your talents and your shortcomings can be an important path to authenticity. When you're aware of your strengths and weaknesses, and when you acknowledge what you don't know, people are more likely to offer their help.

7. **Embrace self-expression.** Don't be afraid to ask questions, speak openly and honestly, and give raise when it's deserved. Giving up a little control over your words might cause people to open up and connect with you.

8. **Collaborate.** Most companies rely on teams of individuals collaborating toward a common goal. Good leaders not only provide guidance and support but are willing to pitch in and help. They also know how to draw out team members' talents and make them feel valued, which in turn, may make them feel more invested in the company's success.

9. **Exude confidence.** Many great leaders have an air of confidence, make decisions quickly and are unafraid of

risk. These things cannot happen if you're hindered by doubt or feelings of inadequacy. Take the steps to build your confidence, which can give you greater control over your life.

10. *Join in extracurricular activities.* Outside activities can help enhance relationships and may enable you to really know other people. Join a team just for the fun of it. You'll be surprised at what you find out about your capabilities.

From Mahatma Gandhi and Winston Churchill, to Martin Luther King and Steve Jobs, there can be as many ways to lead as there are leaders. There is never a one-size-fits-all leadership style for every person and each operate differently. However, understanding various leadership styles enables you to not only adopt the correct characteristics for yourself, but also choose what fits your style best.

Here are nine common leadership styles and famous leaders who have used this type of leadership style:

Transformational Leadership. People who show transformational leadership typically inspire others through effective communication and by creating an environment of intellectual stimulation. Some of the most famous individuals in history are transformational leaders, such as Marcus Aurelius, Richard Branson, and Winston Churchill.

Transactional Leadership. Transactional leadership is focused on establishing a clear chain of command and implementing a carrot and stick approach. It is considered transactional because leaders offer an exchange, they reward good performances, while punishing bad practice. This style includes clear structures and subordinates must follow. A transactional leader values order and structure, such as Vince Lombardi, Bill Gates and Howard Schultz.

Servant Leadership. People who practice servant leadership prefer power-sharing models of authority, prioritizing the needs of their team and encouraging collective decision-making. Servant leaders are categorized as those individuals who lead with a primary focus and putting the needs of others before their own. Examples of famous servant leaders are Mahatma Gandhi, Marin Luther King, Jr., and Mother Teresa.

Autocratic Leadership. Autocratic leaders have significant control over others and rarely consider suggestions or share power. Autocratic leadership is vital in many environments because it demands error-free outcomes. There are many examples of leaders who prefer the "my way or the highway" technique, such as General George Patton, John D. Rockefeller, and Richard M. Nixon.

Laissez-faire Leadership. Laissez-faire literally means "let them do" in French. This is typically translated to "let it be." As such, laissez-faire leaders are characterized by their hands-off approach, allowing others to get on with tasks as they see fit. Providing a minimum level of overall supervision, laissez faire is often employed on a group of individuals who are fully knowledgeable and mature in their field with proven competence. The following are some of the famous laissez faire leaders: Herbert Hoover, Queen Victoria, and Warren Buffet.

Democratic Leadership. Democratic leadership means leaders often ask for input from others before making a final decision. All successful democratic leaders are self-actualizing people with loads of self-confidence. They take responsibility for their actions, they support their team, and they don't make excuses for failures. The most famous democratic leaders in history have been George Washington, Abraham Lincoln, and John F. Kennedy.

Bureaucratic Leadership. Bureaucratic leadership is one of the oldest forms of leadership. It dates back to the first world rulers, including Genghis Khan and Julius Caesar. These leaders governed huge territories, and were forced to create rules, regulation, and hierarchies that were easily replicable. Bureaucratic leaders rely on rules and regulations and clearly defined positions within an organization and they tend to be well organized. Examples of modern bureaucratic leaders are Margaret Thatcher, Steve Jobs, and Colin Powell.

Charismatic Leadership. There is a certain amount of overlap between charismatic and transformational leadership. Both styles rely heavily on the positive charm and personality of the leader. However, charismatic leadership is usually considered less favorable, largely because the success of the outcome is closely linked to the presence of the leader. While transformational leaders build confidence in others. What sets charismatic leaders apart is that they are essentially very skilled communicators, individuals who are both verbally eloquent but also able to communicate to followers on a deep emotional level. Examples of charismatic leaders include, Ronald Reagan, Pope John Paul II, and Napoleon Bonaparte.

Situational Leadership. Developed by management experts Paul Hersey and Ken Blanchard in 1969, situational leadership is a theory that the best leaders utilize a range of different styles, depending on the situation. Situational leadership requires the leader to possess a variety of traits and skills, as the leader must adapt to different situations and to respond accordingly. Examples of situational leaders include, General George Patten, Jack Stahl, and Phil Jackson.

Stepping up and being a leader is an extremely valuable experience for everyone. It helps us to better understand ourselves and the role we wish to play in our lives. It helps us get better in living up to our values and own expectations. Leadership helps us to live our own lives, not the life of others. Leadership is not a role but a mindset and attitude, a behavior, a way of thinking and acting and living, which can produce outstanding outcomes.

World leaders have demonstrated different leaderships and they have been successful in accomplishing various challenging tasks. Some of the common features important for leaders in today's world are creating a vision so that everyone has an idea about the goal that will be achieved; motivating people to make valuable contributions; and developing excellent communication skills so that a clear, concise, and correct message can be communicated to everyone.

I am not a motivational speaker, but I am an action taker. I challenge you to take action now, so you can get closer to owning yourself. The following challenge will help you know how to become a leader.

Take Action Now

Your assignment is to choose a leadership style that works for you and implement it in your business or life.

My Leadership Style:

_____

_____

_____

_____

_____

_____

_____

_____

_____

_____

_____

_____

_____

GO OWN YOURSELF

_____

_____

_____

_____

_____

_____

_____

_____

_____

_____

_____

_____

_____

_____

_____

_____

_____

_____

GO OWN YOURSELF

CHAPTER SEVEN

KNOW HOW TO BECOME SUCCESSFUL

"Here's to the crazy ones. The misfits. The rebels. The troublemakers. The round pegs in the square holes. The ones who see things differently. They're not fond of rules. And they have no respect for the status quo. You can quote them, disagree with them, glorify or vilify them. About the only thing you can't do is ignore them. Because they change things. They push the human race forward. And while some may see them as the crazy ones, we see genius. Because the people, who are crazy enough to think they can change the world, are the ones who do." – Steve Jobs

We all want success. We want to be successful and feel successful. We chase money, fame, power, education, relationships and a hundred other things without ever stopping to ask one essential question: What is success? Before you can pursue success, and success will mean different things to difference people, you need to understand what success means to you. Throughout childhood and early adulthood, we learn various ideas of success from our parents, teachers and friends. Everyone has their own agenda and idea of who and what we should be. Although it is fine to value the opinions of others, we shouldn't necessarily adopt them as our own, so we must set our goals, objectives, and trajectories based on what we desire.

It is essential to understand that in many ways, we already are successful. If we assume that we are failures until we reach a specific goal, we will never be happy. We have to recognize all we have already accomplished and you can start by asking yourself:

Where have I already seen success in life?

How can I continue building on that success?

What lessons have I learned from those successes?

The dictionary defines success as the accomplishment of one's goal; the desired result of an attempt; or one that succeeds. Pop culture would have you think that success is all about money, fame, and power. The truth is, success is going to be what you want it to be. Only you can define your success.

We know if we want to achieve something we have to do something. To be successful, you use each day as an opportunity to improve, to be better, to get a little bit closer to your goals. It might sound like a lot of work and with a busy schedule, next to impossible. But the best part is, the more you accomplish, the more you'll want to do, the higher you'll want to reach. So as long as you have the hunger for success, and success can be whatever you want it to be, you will always have the power within you to achieve it.

So how do we achieve success? Let's start with the basics:

Dream It. Everything begins in the heart and mind. Every great achievement began in the mind of one person. They dared to dream, to believe that it was possible. Think big and accomplish the first step today – dream it.

Believe It. Your dream must be believable. You must be able to say that if you work hard enough, you can accomplish it. Achieving success starts with believing in yourself.

See It. Great achievers have a habit, they see things. They picture themselves doing what they dream of.

Tell It. Tell everyone you encounter about your dream because as we continually say it, we believe it more and more.

Plan It. Every dream must take the form of a plan. The old saying that you "get that you plan for" is very true. Your dream will not just happen, you have to put it into motion with a plan.

Work It. You must work on your dream to see it become reality. Follow the steps of your plan and see your dream take shape and eventually become alive.

Enjoy It. When you have reached your goal and you are living your dream, be sure to enjoy it.

START NOW

Regardless of how old you are, where you live, or what your career goals are, it is likely your ultimate goals in life are to be happy and successful. To be successful means more than just having money and making your mark. It means following your passions, living purposefully, and enjoying the present moment. Here are some actions you can start doing today because they will give you the success you want tomorrow:

Start taking ownership. Most people make excuses or need to blame others when things are not working. But true success happens when you start to take responsibility and stop making excuses; when you start to be accountable and when you stop blaming others. When you start to say, "If it's going to happen, it will happen because I made it happen." Remember, excuses will always be there, but opportunities will not.

Start being more focused. If you want to succeed, stop being distracted by everything around you and be more focused in what you want to achieve. Stay focused on what you must do to get it done. When you focus on what you want, everything else falls away.

Start fighting for what you want. When it comes to succeeding, some will succeed because they are destined to, but most succeed because they fight for what they want. To achieve something significant be fearless in pursuit of what you want to achieve. Even if nobody believes in what you are doing, do what it takes to make it happen. You must be determined, and you must be tenacious. Don't be afraid to give yourself everything you ever wanted in life.

Start engaging with people you admire. Having people you admire and look up to in your life can be a great resource for learning and motivation. Reaching out to successful people you admire and respect is a wise strategy. Start hanging out with people who are dependable and reliability. Always choose relationships based on respect and trust and make sure that their words match their actions and deeds.

Start being more disciplined. Discipline gives us the freedom to put all our focus into achieving our goals.

HABITS OF SUCCESSFUL PEOPLE

When talking about success, keep in mind successful people are those who had a vision of what their impact on the world should be, and made their vision come true. Why recreate the wheel when we don't have to? Let's look at the habits of some of the most successful people and start practicing those habits to achieve your own success.

Habit 1 – Keep learning and read books

You would be amazed at how much time successful people

spend listening to podcasts, watching documentaries, or simply reading books. Most top CEO's read an average of 4 to 5 books a month.

Habit 2 – Be curious and diversify

Many successful people have a variety of different interests and are very curious. When looking at someone like Arnold Schwarzenegger, who became the most renowned body-builder, then a famous actor, and then the Governor of California, it becomes clear that his mental strength was the foundation for his success.

Habit 3 – Step back

While working hard increases your chance of being successful, you can easily fall in the trap of becoming a workaholic. It is more important to work smart. Stepping back will let you analyze what you spend time on actually matters.

Habit 4 – Drive the bus

Successful people are completely in control of the projects they choose, and in control of how they use their time. Many people say they don't have time to do something, but successful people simply prioritize what they do with their time.

Habit 5 – Help people around you

Most of the top achievers in the world understand that helping those around you is not a zero-sum game and that when you help people around you, you create an environment where they give back.

Habit 6 – Focus on what matters and avoid distractions

Successful people recommend you don't try to optimize everything, only the things that matter. You should notice when you are doing something very unproductive, like spending countless hours on social media, as these divert you from the goals you choose for yourself.

Habit 7 – Trust yourself, follow your instincts and be resilient

When you achieve greater harmony and clarity, you should then use your clarity to take action. You should go beyond your rational mind and trust what you know is right, trust that little voice inside of you.

Habit 8 – Learn to say no

Focus is very important, and you need to own your time and projects. So, when you understand that something is not worth pursuing, learn to say no, whether you say no to a request or a job.

Habit 9 – Understand your fears and overcome them

Sometimes you want to do something but find yourself making excuses not to. It can be a good idea when you have this feeling to put the pros and cons on paper and analyze what you should do.

Habit 10 – Start the day with a conquering mindset

Successful people wake up early and have morning routines. The reason behind this is to get excited about the day and start with a feeling of achievement.

Success doesn't just happen to people. You have to do something to make it happen. Most successful people experiment to find out what works for them. No matter where you are in life there is always more to reach for. When you constantly strive to become a better person, refine your skill set and invest in your future daily, you become more as an individual. When you become more as an individual, your value increases. The more your value increases, the more successful you will become and it all starts with your habits. You should adapt your daily habits rather than following other people's routines blindly. The best way to know what works for you is to start experimenting with best practices and adjust them as you go.

I am not a motivational speaker, but I am an action taker. I challenge you to take action now, so you can get closer to owning yourself. The following challenge will help you know how to become successful.

Take Action Now

Your assignment is to list all your successes and take some time to reflect on them. Consider why you chose those successes and what success would you like to achieve.

My Successes:

_____

_____

_____

_____

_____

_____

_____

_____

_____

_____

_____

_____

_____

_____

_____

_____

_____

_____

_____

_____

_____

_____

_____

_____

_____

_____

_____

_____

_____

_____

_____

_____

_____

GO OWN YOURSELF

_____

_____

_____

_____

_____

_____

_____

_____

_____

_____

_____

_____

_____

_____

_____

_____

_____

_____

CHAPTER EIGHT

KNOW HOW TO OWN IT

"History will be kind to me for I intend to write it."
– Winston Churchill

Some people spend much of their lives in unnecessary anguish over what others expect of them. Or worse, they just let life happen to them and follow along passively. The only way you can even begin to start living life on your own terms is to recognize that it's your life and it's time for you to own it.

Let's face facts, the only way you can truly master your own life is if you understand and accept the reality of others. We are all set in our ways. As much as we tout how open-minded we all are, we all have little nitpicks about others. This should not stop you from doing what you want to do, but it also should not come as a surprise when someone tries to tell you you're doing it wrong or you're going to fail. This means that they just noticed you and being noticed is the first step in owning yourself.

Fear can make us afraid of what others will think. It's not a question of if people will judge you, because they definitely will. People are judgmental, it's part of their nature and that judgment can be scary. While we all care what others have to say, it becomes dangerous when we value their opinions more than our own. The second step in owning yourself is to value your own judgment as you are the only person who knows you well.

Being judged and being respected are not the same thing. People can think you are a terrible person and still hold you in high regards. Conversely, if someone judges you as a nice person, it does not mean they respect you. People walk all over nice people all the time, yet people do not tend to walk over people they respect. The good thing about people not respecting you is that you can simply disassociate yourself from them. They will never support you or make you a better person, so you drop them as quickly as possible. If you respect yourself publicly and proudly, chances are others will too. The third step in owning yourself is to respect yourself first, respect what you have done so far in life, and respect what you are going to do in life.

NEVER LET SOMEONE ELSE PICK YOUR PASSION

There is no perfect success formula that exists, believe me, I've looked. Successful people look like they have it all, yet there are too many variables to account for what specifically worked in creating their success. The only difference between them and you is they did not stop at the first hint of failure or roll over and quit. They kept on trying until something worked. If someone tells you that you shouldn't do that or that cannot be done, assume they are talking based on their own experience. Their advice is clouded by their own ideas, their own experiences, and their own choices.

The forth step in owning yourself is to find your passion and chase it to the ends of the earth, if that's what it takes. If something does not work for you, then change the way you are doing it and try something new to achieve your passion. Without passion, what do you truly have?

Research shows that about 40 percent of Americans have not determined a sense of purpose in their lives. It's easy to say "Live life on your own terms", but if you have not figured out those terms, you may feel lost. When you don't know what you want, you are like a ship without a rudder. So, what can you do to ensure that you lead a life that is uniquely meaningful to you? Here are some ways to help you define your terms and start owing yourself:

Recognize your freedom to choose. Living life on your own terms starts with the knowledge that you can do just that, if you so choose. Everything you see around you and every person you make contact with is there because of a choice you made. If you don't like the way your life is, make the choice to change it.

Stand on your own two feet. When you steadily require guidance from those around you, you give up control of how your life plays out. Always maintain control of your life. Even when you ask for advice from others, thoughtfully consider their suggestions, but always be the one who makes the final decision.

Access your values. Who you are as a person, what kind of people you surround yourself with, what you do for a living, what you are passionate about, all of these are guided by your personal values. Learn what your values are by taking any personal values assessment, which you can find online. Understanding your values helps you grasp a deeper understanding of yourself, what motivates you, and what your dreams are.

Dream big. As you move toward living life on your own terms, you must get a handle on exactly what that means to you. Write down all your dreams, which will help you uncover what it is you really want out of your life.

Let go of expectations set by others. This can be a difficult practice, especially if you have lived a life governed by others. Trust your instincts. If you know what your core values are then you can trust your own decision-making skills. If you know your values and what you want to reflect in your life, then you have no reason to look to others for validation.

Stop comparing. Comparing yourself to someone else puts your focus on them instead of on yourself, where it should be.

95

Instead of comparing yourself to others, try to measure yourself against where you were last month, six months ago, or even a year ago.

Set specific goals with deadlines that challenge you. You may have heard that you should set SMART goals: specific, measurable, achievable, results-focused, and time-bound. Develop an action plan to meet these goals with clear and measurable steps.

Do one thing daily that moves you closer to achieving your goals. If you are truly serious about living a life on your own terms, then you must be responsible for prioritizing your goals. Each week make sure the first tasks you perform each day are those with the highest priority.

Spend time with people who inspire, uplift, and value you. Your life can be enhanced by the people who surround you. You cannot expect to see positive changes in your life when you spend most of your time with negative people. Positive energy coming from your friends and loved ones gives you greater confidence, reduces stress, and makes you happier.

Take chances. Get out there and collect experiences. Taking even small risks helps you to build confidence in yourself and your abilities. Taking chances also helps you better learn how to navigate different obstacles and refine your abilities.

Learn from your mistakes. Don't think too long on your mistakes other than finding ways to learn from them. You often learn the most when you are out in an uncomfortable situation. Failure is only temporary so use your losses to help you become better so the next risk results in a win.

MAKE YOUR CHOICES WITH COURAGE AND CONFIDENCE

If you choose to confront the options before you with courage and confidence, you open yourself to a fulfilling path of your own design, filled with numerous possibilities. Rather than procrastinate in fear of making the wrong decision, weigh your options and act on the best one, and revel in the chance to create the life you want to live.

Is it a big deal to live to be 100 and don't actually do anything during that time? It's better to live 40 years packed full of things that make life worth living. Don't worry about the years that have gone by, worry about filling your remaining years with the life you want to live. When you truly own it, you can enjoy all your life moments no matter what you are doing or where you are.

"Everyone is born with the potential for greatness. What happens next is up to you. You get to choose which path you take, how high to set the bar for yourself, and how hard you're willing to work to clear it. You get to decide how to spend your time, who to spend it with, and what you're willing to forgo when time runs short. Every choice that you make and every action that you take has consequences, but who better to decide what's best for you – than you. It's your life to live. Own it!" – Frank Sonnenberg.

I am not a motivational speaker, but I am an action taker. I challenge you to take action now, so you can get closer to owning yourself. The following challenge will help you with knowing how to own it.

Take Action Now

Your assignment is to list one goal you have yet to accomplish. Ask yourself if this goal truly belongs to you or are you trying to achieve someone else's goal.

My Goal:

_____

_____

_____

_____

_____

_____

_____

_____

_____

_____

_____

_____

_____

_____

_____

_____

_____

_____

_____

_____

_____

_____

_____

_____

_____

_____

_____

_____

_____

_____

_____

_____

_____

_____

_____

_____

CHAPTER NINE

KNOW YOUR RESOURCES

"Success is not about your resources. It's about how resourceful you are with what you have." — Tony Robbins

The lessons shared in this book can be applied to nearly every aspect of your life. The intention was to help you own yourself so you can own your business with confidence. Remember, people like to do business with people who are confident. There are more entrepreneurs now than ever before and the ones that actually make it to success are the ones that own themselves. Maybe owning your own business is one of your dreams, it certainly was mine. Maybe you just need a push in the right direction, and maybe you are looking for resources to help you.

The 21st century has brought great new opportunities for entrepreneurs. However, the world is also moving faster than ever and the competition is massive, so you have to gain every advantage you can get to turn your passion into a sustainable business.

How smartly you use your time and how productively you tap into your resources determines how successful you become. As you start your journey to own yourself, you will need the help of professionals who understand what it takes to be successful.

Let today be the day you chase your dream and actually put things into motion. Start by listing your own resources, such as:

- Your connections
- Your business advisor
- Your financial advisor
- Your lawyer
- Your accountant
- Your banker

If you have not yet created a relationship with the professionals listed above, I'll be happy to share mine as I have spent years trying to find the best in the business and I cherish each one.

Here is a list of my best resources:

1. Accountant
   Guerin CPA
   www.californiacpafirm.com

2. Financial Advisor
   Wealthspring Financial Planners LLC
   www.wealthspringfp.com

3. Legal
   Bagla Law Firm, APC
   www.baglalaw.com

4. Business Coach
   On Track Success Coaching
   www.ontracksuccesscoaching.com

5. Business Insurance
   H. Linwood Insurance Services, Inc.
   www.hlinwood-insurance.com

6. Bookkeeping
   Jes Taxes, Inc.
   www.jestaxes.com

7. Marketing
   All Maven
   www.allmaven.com

8. Media
   One Productions
   www.oneproductionsweb.com

9. Branding
   Snap Savvy Strategies
   www.snapsavvystrategies.com

10. Graphic Designer
    Kate Brand Design
    www.katebranddesign.com

11. Personal Stylist
    Lyndell Werling
    www.lyndellwerling.com

12. Personal Trainer
    Diamond Body Fitness

https://www.facebook.com/diamondbodyfit/

I am not a motivational speaker, but I am an action taker. I
challenge you to take action now, so you can get closer to owning

yourself. The following challenge will help you with knowing your resources.

Take Action Now

Your assignment is to list all your resources and make appointments with them to start the ball rolling.

My Resources:

_____

_____

_____

_____

_____

_____

_____

_____

_____

_____

_____

_____

_____

_____

_____

_____

GO OWN YOURSELF

GO OWN YOURSELF

CHAPTER TEN

MY REFLECTIONS

Writing this book has been truly a pleasure and an eye-opening experience. I am a person that always knew I was made for greater things. It's a feeling deep down that keeps knocking and hoping one day you'll open the door. I am not a physiatrist or a theorist and I don't hold advance degrees in human behavior. What I am is a person who has shared her experiences with you. I wasn't born with confidence, I learned it. I wasn't born a leader, I stepped into that role and claimed it. I wasn't born to own it, I followed my passion and now live the life I love.

I was one of those people who associated success with money. I thought that only rich people were successful and that they were born to be successful. Little did I know that everyone is born with the same capabilities, for the most part, to become as successful as they want. Success really has nothing to do with money. The day I graduated from law school, I was successful. The day I started work for the largest international law firm in the world, I was successful. The day I opened my own law firm, I was successful. The day I met my husband, I was successful. The day I experienced the love of a dog, I was successful. The day my clients gave me the title: 'Queen of Business Law', I was successful. The day I wrote this book, I was successful.

It's not how others define success to be, it's what you define success to be. Living the life you want is achievable but you have to make changes, work hard, and celebrate all the successes you accomplish. Give it a try. You have nothing to lose but everything to gain. I would like to leave you with this beautiful thought that sums up my whole book – Go Own Yourself!

A Promise of Success
By Michael Sage

One's potential is so huge, and so vast,

Yet, why is it, that so many fail, and usually come last?

So few truly succeed, that when they do, others are jealous and totally aghast.

Let's all believe in success, and I promise that failure will be part of the past.

The things you think, and the things you believe,

If they are true, then those are the things that you will achieve.

You'll be stabbed in the back, and that is a promise that you had better believe.

Get rid of depression, worry and fear,

Because success is so often so very, very near.

Tell your subconscious, "Success is mine," and tell it to hear.

Remind it often, then success will be yours, that is a promise, my dear.

Just ask the "DIVINE" for whatever you desire.

For happiness or abundance, or anything else to which you aspire.

It's now time to succeed, so go ahead, set your goals, and light that fire.

Do it with passion, and I promise you this, you'll soar higher and higher.

Thank You!

Thank you for reading **Go Own Yourself!** I hope you found the information useful to put you on the road to owning your world.

If you are starting a new business, or working to grow an existing one, you may also want to read <u>Go Legal Yourself!</u> where I present the Legal Lifecycle of your business and how you can easily move from one phase to the next, from Startup to Growth, or from Establishment to Exit.

You can find useful information for starting your business and an easy to use template for a business plan, among other legal business packages, on my Go Legal Yourself website: <u>www.golegalyourself.com</u>.

Another useful resource for learning quick tips and hearing some incredible stories from successful business people, please download my Go Legal Yourself podcast app from your app store.

Remember knowledge is POWER!

GO OWN YOURSELF

ABOUT THE AUTHOR

KELLY BAGLA, ESQ.

Kelly Bagla, Esq. is an experienced author, speaker, business owner and corporate attorney who practices in San Diego, California. As the Queen of Business Law®, Kelly is not your average attorney.

After a successful career as a corporate and securities attorney for the world's strongest global law firm, Kelly founded Bagla Law Firm, APC.

Having worked for the largest law firm in the world, with some of the best legal minds in business (along with her impressive education), Kelly has acquired a wealth of information on what it takes to make and run a successful business.

She lives her passion everyday by doing what she loves and that is advising business owners on how to know and leverage each of the four phases of the legal lifecycle of their business and educating people about how to succeed as business entrepreneurs.

Understanding the legal aspects of a business is essential for any business to succeed, no matter what phase they're in. With a solid legal foundation for your business, there's no limit to what you can achieve!

Kelly wrote "Go Legal Yourself!" as a way to finally empower business owners with the best information there is on how to launch, grow and sustain their business legally! By creating the "4 Legal Lifecycles" of a business, Kelly broke down how to start, grow, establish and exit a business into 4 easy steps that will make any business bullet proof and extremely successful!

She has a long list of impressive domestic and international clients who have deemed her **"Queen of Business Law®"** and for good reason. She's tough as nails, smooth as silk, and determined to make your business successful!

Kelly has been recognized for her work in some very prestigious publications, such as LA Dreams Magazine, Inventor's Digest and California Business Journal to name a few.

She's madly in love with her Marine husband and their three beautiful dogs. (If dogs could own businesses, she'd help them too!)

To learn more about Kelly Bagla and Bagla Law Firm, APC, visit her website at <u>www.Baglalaw.com</u>.

Take Action Now

If you enjoyed Go Own Yourself and found it useful, please take a moment to write a review on Amazon. Thank You!

Made in the USA
Columbia, SC
15 August 2018